How to S
Unique Data Entry
Business
From Home

A Guide For Those Individuals Seeking To Start A One Of A Kind Business For Themselves

g crutcher dutch

DEDICATION

This book is dedicated to my deceased parents. Without their support and encouragement throughout life, this book would not have been possible and to the people who have worked in offices and now wish to use their skills to enrich their own lives with freedom.

TABLE OF CONTENT

TERMS AND CONDITIONS

FORWARD

Do you want to start your own business? In our society each of us has the opportunity to create a business. If you've picked up this book, you no doubt have the motivation. And you need the information this book can provide.

We all know that it is small businesses that create jobs, provide services, strengthen communities, and is a critical factor in a person's road to prosperity.

Yet this book will take a step beyond the phrase "small business" and look at a particular type of small business - what I call a data entry business specifically for churches. Now the challenge is to bring you forth into this productive and unique type of data entry business.

This book is designed as a guide for those individuals seeking to be in business for themselves and those existing business persons searching for new opportunities.

INTRODUCTION

If you are considering starting a home-based business you may want to consider data entry. This book focuses on a particular type of data entry business specifically designed for churches. This type of business is growing in leaps and bounds, and for good reason. Data entry is clearly one line of work that has seen significant changes in recent years and as online work becomes more common and resources become tighter, churches are realizing the benefits of outsourcing many data entry tasks. Today, the technology is considered reliable, safe and secure.

Churches are businesses too and they are susceptible to economic hardships and shrinking revenues. A reduction in expenses helps churches greatly as operating costs are skyrocketing and contributions are dwindling. The idea of keeping full-time staff on board is not feasible for churches anymore. Data entry is particularly appealing for outsourcing as it is easily controlled and it can be done outside of church hours. Data input may be done day or night, regardless of the day of the year. Outsourcing data entry can also be very advantageous when there are time zone differences as the contractor may do the work while the client is sleeping. Consequently, it is already one of the most outsourced jobs on the information super highway, and that's not going to change. In fact, many surveys suggest that up to 65% of data entry work will be handled by independent contractors, many from the comfort of their own home. As businesses worldwide feel the squeeze of the new economic climate, more and more will turn to remote businesses to provide their services. Many businesses simply cannot afford to keep even part-time staff due to financial stresses.

Clearly, now is a great time to get in on the ground floor of a business like this. Plus, data entry management for churches does not require huge amounts of capital nor endless degrees behind your name. You can start with a minimum amount of investment, a reasonable amount of training and a very small space in your home. Naturally, you will need organizational skills, accuracy and the will to succeed.

HOW MUCH POTENTIAL?

The possibilities for a home-based data entry business are almost unlimited. One has only to look at how online work has grown over the past decade to see that it is going to grow exponentially in the future. Business support services will grow – there is no doubt. They are fulfilling a need in the marketplace and that need will not diminish any time soon. In fact, it is likely to continue growing as more functions are computerized and cloud-based technologies flourish making data management easier and more accessible.

Today, churches are finding that they need to track more data on more activities in order to stay afloat. In addition, administrative demands may no longer be limited to a single ministry. Church data may transcend cities or states, and sometimes even reach around the world. Many ministries connect to other locations for missionary work, fundraising or other church business and all of this data needs to be tracked.

Good database management plays a crucial role in the success of any church. Accurate reporting insures proper budgeting for future events and real time analysis of current funds. Churches cannot afford to ignore their data as it is the backbone of their operation. Churches must be able to keep on top of the flow of information and the method must be simple and easy to use. Hiring someone else to set up the forms and systems to capture data is a popular option as it allows staff to concentrate on the good works that want to see come to completion, not the day to day work that tends to bog them down.

This book will explore many ideas that you may not have considered and it may answer many of the questions you have about this type of business. Your potential for success is high if you do your due diligence, plan wisely and approach your business with common sense and patience. Perhaps more importantly, starting a remote data entry business has the added advantage of being very economical. You need not break the bank to get your business up and running. You can start small and watch your business grow over time.

WHY CHURCH DATA ENTRY?

Data management for churches is an excellent niche market with over 450,000 churches in the United States alone. The acceptance of remote work as a normal business practice also means that you are not limited to just the U.S. Any English speaking country is fair game for an online church data entry business which makes it a small business with almost unlimited potential for growth and profit.

What makes churches so appealing? Besides their numbers, there will be many near to you and they may not even know about this type of service as it is not all that common, yet. You may already have some kind of connection to your local church, so this is an excellent opportunity to explore how you might be able to help them. Generally, churches are looking at someone to enter and organize the huge amounts of data they need into a useable form. In many ways, your job is to make the church run smoother and to free up others to do what they really want to do within the church. The data remains the property of the church, but you provide them with the forms to record the information and then do the data entry.

WHY WORK FROM HOME?

Good reasons for working from home are many and varied. In recent years, one of the primary motivators for starting a home-based business is the lack of job security in the marketplace. Big corporations have embraced outsourcing with a vengeance and now many data entry jobs go to foreign workers. Fortunately, church work is still a relatively untapped market and you have a particularly distinct advantage if you live and work in the area.

Having a home office means you do not have to pay for an extra space and extra furniture for an area that you would only use for a portion of each day. Working from home reduces overhead and it allows you to price your products and services in a more competitive manner while retaining personalized service, which is often so lacking today.

On a personal level, the reasons for working from home are many. Many people are tired of battling traffic every day to get to a job where they feel under-appreciated and often times, underpaid. Other people realize that they could make far more money if they simply did the work themselves instead of working for someone else. Far more people just get tired of the rat race and want to take their future into their own hands.

Whatever your reasons for considering a home-based business, data entry for churches has great potential and the promise of a decent income. While any business takes time to establish, once you have a relationship with a church it will likely be long-term. As well, chances are that you will be treated fairly if you do your job well.

WHAT WILL I BE DOING?

Churches collect huge amounts of data and never seem to have enough people to handle it. Your job will be to set up systems to collect data on a timely basis so that it provides beneficial, usable data to the church. This data may include membership data such as names, addresses, telephone numbers, email addresses, family connections, donations and church activities, to name just a few. Your job will be to create and manage all of the information in the database so it easily accessible and simple to manipulate.

The church may also ask you to perform other duties associated with the data such as producing reports, sending emails or letters, managing finances or soliciting for donations on behalf of the church or any other manner of administrative work. As a business owner, it will be up to you to negotiate the terms of your responsibilities and establish what expectations each church has from your work.

WHAT'S INCLUDED IN A CHURCH DATABASE?

Church databases are often more about connections than lists. While every church wants to know who their current members are, they may also want to know who belongs in their family, whether they belong to any special interest groups and perhaps even how much they have donated throughout the year. A church database may contain all of the usual information that you would expect to see in a database, plus much more personal data.

The principle data will include all church members in one easy to access location. Their information may be as detailed as the church wishes including their photos, basic contact information, groups, skills and certifications as well as volunteer activities. Family profiles are also connected to this data so that correspondence goes to one family member, rather than everyone in the family. Family details may include birthdates and special talents such as musical, athletic or artistic abilities.

Group data can also be tracked to see who's doing what within the church and community. Group data can be extremely specific so that you can narrow down who to contact about any specific activity or follow-up such as interested in membership, volunteering, need assistance, etc. The database can also be used to trigger email responses to particular situations.

Databases have become very sophisticated, which makes them incredibly powerful tools. As an owner of a home-based church data entry business, you have the opportunity to tailor this software for each individual church and learn as you go.

Once you have all the information regarding the church members into your database, impress your clients with the perfect letter or email for their members in minutes. With just a few clicks of your mouse, you can have access to 900 letters that will enhance your data entry business for churches. Go to http://www.mychurchletters.com/. Select from a wide range of letters for any of the following situations and simply fill in your personal information and the letter is ready to go. Plus, each letter can be easily edited or personalized to fit your specific needs.

Absences • Announcements • Apologies • Appointments • Birthdays • Church Membership • Community • Condolences • Congratulations • Donations and Fundraisers • Employment • Encouragement • Evangelism • Facilities • Finances • Funerals • Get Well • Guest Ministries • Holidays • Invitations • Marriages • Minister Appreciation • Missions • Music Ministries • Pastor Appreciation Day • Recommendations • Revivals • Small Groups • Sunday School • Thank You's • Vacation Bible School • Visitors • and Youth Letters.

BEFORE YOU START

Financial Considerations

Starting your own business is an exciting time and the decision to jump in with both feet is exhilarating. However, knowing whether an opportunity is right for you takes time, investigation and a level head.

Few businesses earn great deals of money from the very moment they open their doors. As a result, many operators start their businesses on the side while working full-time jobs so their personal living expenses are covered. If you are anxious to get started, make sure you have savings set aside to tide you over until your business starts to turn a profit. Most entrepreneurial guides suggest you should have a minimum of three months savings in the bank as a safety net. This is a bare minimum and it is likely you will want far more than this. Six months to a year of savings will certainly let you sleep better at night.

Starting a business takes much more than money. It also includes educating yourself in what it takes to keep your business running, even when times are tough. Most new businesses do not survive because the owners haven't bothered to think ahead. If the economy does a downturn they are sunk. This need not be the case though.

If a business owner learns fiscal responsibility from the onset of their business, their practices will become habit and the chances of failure will be far less. Responsibility includes analyzing the affordability of purchases and resisting impulse buying. You may want that brand new, high speed computer that is the latest and greatest thing on the market, but can you really afford it? You must examine each prospective purchase and determine whether you truly need it and whether or not the money is being spent in the wisest manner. Everyone has bought something on the spur of the moment because it makes them feel good but when you own a business you need to know that what you buy will increase your profitability. When you spend money on frivolous purchases you pull resources away from the areas of your business that could have used those funds to earn for you.

If you are planning to run your business on your own, the decisions are all up to you. However, if you are contemplating a partnership or a small group working together, make sure you lay out a policy for purchases. You must make sure everyone is on the same page when it comes to spending. Most of us know someone that spends money like it is going out of style and then wonders why they are in debt. You certainly don't want that to be the case with a business partner.

If you have decided to make a major purchase make sure that your business can survive without the money in the bank. You never know what is going to happen so it's best to err on the side of caution. If you absolutely need to buy something to move ahead in your business, by all means do it. Just make sure you do your homework first.

One particularly good tactic for insuring your survival is establishing your credit at your local bank. When times are good, take out a small loan and then pay it back on time. The borrowed money can be placed in an interest bearing investment so it is protected and your bank will begin to recognize you as a reliable business. You will increase your borrowing power and this may be crucial to fall back on should an emergency arise.

Even if you are on a budget when you start you do not have to look it. Make sure that whatever you do, you do well or simply don't do it all. No one will look at marketing materials if they are shoddy and full of errors. Use outsourcing to your advantage if you do not have the skills.

If you have obtained administrative diplomas or certificates, be sure to mention them in your literature and display them in your office. This is a world where credentials mean a lot and when you are trying to entice a remote client, anything you can do to overcome their fear of working with a stranger will help you. Clients want to know that you are prospering because you are competent. If you have past testimonials from people you have worked with, even while you were working for somebody else, use them to your advantage. You never know who knows who and a personal endorsement can open doors in ways that no brochure ever will.

TRAINING AND EDUCATION

Software

To get started in a church data entry business, you must master the software skills that it requires. These skills not only include data entry but word processing and spreadsheets as well. If you are already doing administrative work you likely have a working knowledge of Microsoft Excel and Microsoft Word. For those of you that do not you have several options.

One of the most popular learning methods today is online. Course material is very reasonable as an instructor is not required and you can study at your own pace. Materials may include videos, workbooks, question and answer tests and even certification. You can also self-educate with the help of books you can buy from Amazon or through many free tutorials available on YouTube or from www.office.Microsoft.com and https://support.office.com. Some books include a student version of the software that allows you to install it on your computer and follow along with the lessons. These books may also have online resources such as answers to tests in the textbook together with explanations on how the answers were derived. This can be a very effective way to find out if you have grasped a concept or not.

While the majority of us can relate to word processing because we use it in so many ways today, spreadsheets can be a totally different matter. Fortunately, an effective Excel database need not be too complex if it is set up correctly from the start. It should be simple enough for any new person to figure out, yet be effective enough that data can be input quickly.

Microsoft Office Excel is the industry standard for spreadsheets because it does so many things and the data can be moved from one program into another with ease. It can be used to calculate formulas, create complex graphs and store unlimited amounts of data. A database is basically a grid that allows you to enter unique data in each row and column. The beauty of a program like Excel is that it allows you to sort, group, and omit data when you want to generate a report. This makes it ideal for finding out who's doing what, where, when and sometimes even why. This is obviously a desirable feature for any church.

Excel's compatibility with Microsoft Word makes creating a mail out a breeze as it can take the data, drop it into a letter and then produce a mailing label. There are many other word processing programs available, but few work together as well.

If you would like formal training, use a recognized college or academy. There is no blanket standard of educational requirements to be a data entry consultant. Educational requirements may be as simple as a high school diploma with additional administrative courses, including Word and Excel. Most online virtual assistant programs are lacking and there is no nationally accredited virtual assistant training certification. Your money is better spent at your local community college or you can get free tutorials online from Microsoft https://support.office.com/en-us/excel.

The bottom line is that if you want to have a business of this nature you need to be able to do the work. Yours clients may have basic demands but they can just as easily want you to really manipulate their data to maximize its benefit to them. You really need to know your software well or have the determination to learn something if you don't know how to do it. Once you get your first client you will want to provide a reliable and efficient service. You can then ask for referrals or testimonials to validate the quality of your work.

Necessary Traits

Data entry is not for everyone. You must be able to sort through data quickly and efficiently and have the ability to put it in some order with ease.

• You must have above average attention to detail as small mistakes can cause big problems.
• You must be willing to learn and keep up with changing technologies.

• You will need excellent communication skills as your business will depend on finding out what the church wants and then making it happen.

• Data entry requires logistical skills and the ability to multitask.

• Your typing skills should be 70 words per minute (wpm) or higher.

• You should have proficient language skills, including grammar and composition.

• You should be familiar with general business practices including how to write proper correspondence and emails as well as telephone protocol.

If you know that you are lacking in any of these things, brush up before you even think of starting. Your superior skills will ensure that clients are happy and increase your chances of getting more business. If you feel your skills are sufficient, that's great. Don't forget that you need to have people skills too. You will need to have a strong, decisive personality and the ability to interact with all types of personalities. Working with the public can be very challenging at times and having good interpersonal skills can strengthen your work relationship with the church. There are courses taught on just about anything you need to know so be open-minded and focused. Being prepared increases your chances of success.

BUSINESS RECORDS

So your skills are up-to-date and you have your hopes set on the future in your new business. That's great. Now we will focus on the business aspect.

Before you lift a finger to design a form or key in one piece of data, you need to think about how you will keep track of all aspects of your business. Your business will sell your services or products and in exchange you will be compensated. You need to know how this money flows in and out of your business and for what.

While not crucial to a home-based business, accounting is certainly not a bad thing to have under your belt if you want to make sure it works. Understanding debits and credits, assets and liabilities and expenses versus revenues makes a lot of sense if you want to make informed decisions. Many business owners find that the level of detail they want from their accounting is beyond their means and they hire a bookkeeper. Others find the daily management of their money crucial to a successful operation and wouldn't have it any other way. A third option is to handle bookkeeping in-house and then send the data to an accountant to review and produce financial statements.

Whatever route you choose, it must be in place before you start so you can track your income and expenses, what you owe other people, and what other people owe you. You will need to set up ways to send reports for taxes and make payments when they are due. If you will have employees you will need to have a payroll system in place too.

INVENTORY AND SALES

If you will be using stock to produce your products you will also need to have a system in place to make sure it gets re-ordered and how much. You will also need a way of estimating how much each customer uses and where you will buy your stock. Do you know if you can get credit from your suppliers?

You may be selling services or products or both. You will need to know how to sell to your customers or you may need to hire someone who can. If you are thinking of doing it yourself, consider what you like in a salesperson and what makes them successful at what they do.

MAINTAINING BUSINESS RELATIONS

Even though you are selling a product or service, you will be a consumer as well. You will need to cultivate a relationship with salespeople but have the ability to say 'no' when it is unreasonable.

Salespeople want to sell and they will try to do so all of the time. Listen patiently, be polite but be firm. When business is booming you may well buy a new model of equipment or a new line of supplies and if you want to get a reasonable deal always treat these people with respect.

If you will be working in a partnership or group business, take the time to establish company policies that reflect your way of thinking, including spending. Accountants provide a valuable service as they can help you to monitor how well you are doing on recouping your original investment and they can also provide you with reports to help you plan your future.

Regular financial reporting is important to identify problems and rectify them before they get out of hand.

EMPLOYEES

You may want to handle the management portion of your business and hire an employee to do some of the other tasks. This is likely once your business grows as you will simply have too much to do. Consider your options for finding competent staff. Have you identified the qualities and skills that they would need to be effective in your company? Have you set aside time for orientation and training and calculated for the loss of revenues while you are doing this?

CREDIT FOR CUSTOMERS

There are not too many customers who pay cash nowadays and most businesses expect to be granted 30 days to pay for your services. However, some customers will honor this agreement and others may not. Most successful businesses extend credit with interest to their prime customers only. Have you figured out the criteria for your credit policy and the pros and cons to it all?

What do you do when a client does not pay, particularly when it's a church? Do you have a method for following up on delinquent accounts that respects your clients and honors your pocketbook? Don't let your accounts receivables list grow. Try to get on top of your invoices as soon as they go past due. Many times it can be an oversight. When it isn't, collecting money can be a bit of an art. The secret is to be pleasant but firm. Most times you will find that you will get at least a partial payment and a promise date for the balance.

PERSONAL CONSIDERATIONS

Being an entrepreneur presents different challenges than working for someone else and it is important that you take a hard look at your personality to see if it is a fit. Consider these questions:

Do you want your own business badly enough to keep you working long hours without knowing how much money you'll end up with?

Are you a self-starter?
Do you get along with people?
Can you make decisions?
Can you lead others?
Can you take responsibility?
Are you a good organizer?
How hard are you willing to work?
Are you trustworthy?
Do you finish what you start?
Have you worked in a business like the one you want to start?
Have you worked for someone else as a foreman or manager?
Have you had any business training in the past?

Have you figured out what net income per year you expect to get from the business? Count your salary and your profit on the money you put into the business.

Can you live on less than this so that you can use some of it to help your business grow?

Are you physically capable of doing the job?

ADDITIONAL ITEMS TO CONSIDER

Have you talked to a banker about your plans?

Have you talked to a lawyer about it?

Do you know the good and bad points about going it alone, having a partner, and incorporating your business? Do you want a partner? Who? How would you split the duties and responsibilities?

Are there data entry businesses in your area? How are they doing? Can you compete or will you need to work in another area?

What about other people in your life? Are they willing to help you if you can't work for some reason? Would they be willing to learn your business? Would they be willing to work in your business with you for at least three or four weeks per year to get to know it? Would they be willing to meet your attorney, accountant, any advisors or consultants, creditors and your major suppliers?

Have you figured out whether or not you could make more money working for someone else? Have you got what it takes to get started?

GETTING STARTED

Congratulations, you've made a commitment and you want to start. Making that decision is one of the major stepping stones in creating a successful business. You have taken the time to improve yourself and you have taken the time to consider all of the factors that could affect the success of your business. This is so important. Now the actual work begins.

Where to start? Right in your own neighborhood is good. Drive around your local area and write down all the churches you see and do an internet search too. Some churches may not look like churches and you may miss them by just looking. Start your first Excel spreadsheet and include any pertinent data you think you may need to contact them. This could be their address for a letter and brochure, their email for an introductory email or their telephone number to set up an appointment to make a personal visit. Always get a contact name if you can and figure out how you are going to proceed. Be systematic and thorough. There may be a lot of needy churches out there that want to hire you. You just have to let them know that you exist. Try www.flockfinder.com, www.usachurch.com, and www.CBN.com.

If you are a sole proprietor you can expect to spend at least one-fourth of your time on general business management and administration, marketing, purchasing and billing. The bigger your business, the more time you'll spend managing rather than actually doing the work yourself but you will still work. When you start out, you will obviously be spending the majority of your time on marketing and advertising to bring in new clients. Advertising can be as simple as a flyer or brochure while marketing requires a plan of action.

Running a data entry business requires a lot of energy, particularly in the beginning. You want new customers, but when you get them you have less time for marketing. You'll need to be able to juggle several projects at the same time, always maintain accuracy and timeliness and do all of it while making customers feel valued and unique. You will need all your skills to pull it off, but you are prepared.

YOUR HOME OFFICE

Of course you can rent an office, buy some furniture and throw a sign on the door if you want to, but does it make sense? Some business owners do opt for an office for various reasons and some of these might apply to you.

• My home is too small for an office.

• It will be too expensive to turn the space I have into a functional office.

• My home is too inaccessible because there is no parking.

• I cannot have a home office because it is against zoning bylaws.

If the space you have set aside seems suitable you must create an area that is conducive to work. It should be separate from your living space and use equipment that is dedicated to your business. Too often, home offices become places for kids to do homework or neighbors to drop by and gab when you are trying to get something done.

If you have a family, establish signals that let them know when you are working and do not want to be disturbed. This is not mean; this is essential. This can be as simple as a 'Do Not Disturb' sign or a closed door.

As well, hook up a dedicated land line for your business that is also off limits to the family. Keep your bills separate, when possible, from household costs and set hours to work for yourself. Your clients will likely expect you to be available during regular business hours but if this is not possible, make it clear when you are available and how. Many remote businesses operate using email and Skype almost exclusively.

STARTUP COSTS

Home-based businesses are very attractive as they have relatively low startup costs and a remote data entry business for a church is no different. While it is possible to borrow to buy the necessary equipment to start earning money, it is far better to have your own startup capital. If this is your first shot at running a business you would have to borrow against your personal credit and need a good credit rating to do so. No bank is going to lend you money unless you can prove that you can pay it back and that's hard to do when you are new to the game. The obvious choice is to use your own savings and your own equipment to start out.

Most data entry businesses start out as part-time ventures as operators run them on the side while working full-time jobs. This is a good way of making sure that your monthly living expenses are paid while slowly adding clients and extra income. As mentioned previously, you should have at least three months of savings (preferably six months to a year) of savings if you want to go at it full-time.

Regardless of which approach you use, sit down with a calculator and list what you are going to need and how you are going to obtain money. Things to consider are equipment, telephone, furniture and supplies. You need to have a plan to stay on track. If the numbers come up short, cross things off your list until you come up with do-able numbers. Obviously, the part-time solution makes a lot of sense as you can earn while you learn. You may discover you do not like the work and want to try something else. You may find out you love it and want to accelerate your plans to get out of your other employment.

The point is it's a wonderful way to test the waters and make some extra cash on the side. You will also be firming up your connections with the churches and establishing your company's reliability. These two factors are critical for the success of your business down the road.

EQUIPMENT AND SUPPLIES

You'll need top-notch equipment to do a top-notch job. Fortunately, computers have become more powerful and getting what you need to run a data entry business need not be expensive. If you are a frugal shopper you may be able to start with as little as $1,000, but $2,000 is more likely. Your equipment, and of course your business savvy, are the prime money-earners for your business so don't skimp out on something that you will use day in and day out for years. Concentrate on quality and durability, especially for your keyboard and printer. These are the work horses of data entry and they should be well-built and reliable.

Hardware

Computer – your computer should have the biggest hard drive you can afford and the highest speed processor. You will be crunching big numbers so a slow computer is a big no-no. Most modern computers, including laptops, are capable of blazing speeds and have enormous hard drives so this is rarely an issue. If you have a computer that is over five years old, consider upgrading or replacing your existing computer. Software changes quickly and the last thing you want is to find out that you have to upgrade because your software is no longer supported. It is better to spend money on your own terms and anticipate the growth of your company.

Multi-function Printer – technology has combined the printer, scanner, fax and copier into one easy-to-use, affordable machine. Define your requirements and research your machine thoroughly before you buy. You may start out with an ink jet printer, but you will soon find that cartridges can be pricey and they are notoriously slow for big jobs. Consider a color laser printer instead. Some companies will lease these to you at a reasonable price which includes service and toner cartridges. You are charged by the number of copies you print. If you want to buy instead, make sure it prints quickly and that the toner is reasonably priced.

Bundled Packages – selling computer equipment as a package is very popular today. Vendors can increase their sales and you can often get something for nothing, or next to nothing, thrown in on the sale. Great sources for these deals are big box stores and online giants like Amazon.

High speed Internet Connection – working remotely means speed matters. Pay for the best connection you can get within your budget and make sure that your provider has a reputation for reliability and service. If your service goes out, you want to be able to find out why and when it will be restored.

Telephone line – if you are serious about this as a business, treat it like a business. Pay for a dedicated landline in the name of your company and get it listed in the telephone directory. There's no use running a business that no one can find.

Software

You do not need a lot of expensive software to start your data entry business but you do need to keep it current. Software upgrades include additions and improvements to programs so that they can work with the latest technologies. You certainly don't want to be left behind because you didn't want to spend the minimal amount on an upgrade. Unfortunately, upgrades happen far too often but it is a cost of doing business and can be used as a business deduction. Here is a basic list of what you will need:

Spreadsheet Software – without a doubt, the industry standard is Microsoft Excel. It is powerful and designed to work with other Microsoft products such as Word, PowerPoint, and Publisher. It is reasonably priced and supported if you have problems.

Word Processing Software – once again, Microsoft is the leader here. Word is powerful and indispensible for moving data out of Excel and into documents. While there are other free word processing programs, such as Open Office, they will never match Word for its compatible functions. Word is also reasonably priced and supported if you have problems.

Fax Software – even though most printers have a fax machine built into them nowadays, you may want to move into the electronic world for your faxes. These services allow you to send faxes through email and save considerable time and effort. The big names are eFax.com, myFax.com, and srfax.com.

Package Deals – there are many vendors that offer package deals where hardware is already loaded with software when you buy it. Make sure that the disc is supplied with the equipment or you have access to the software should you have problems and need to re-install it.

Data Backup – your data is your livelihood, so backup off site is vital. You can purchase cloud storage space at a minimal cost and backup at least daily.

Other Considerations

Buy Used – you can often find second-hand equipment at a fraction of the cost.

Outside Print Services – if you have large print jobs or you do a lot of faxing, you can use outside services in your own business. Bulk print services have made it incredibly easy to use them. You simply upload the file, indicate the format and the quantity and bam, it arrives on your doorstep. Some churches have their own account with a print service and you need only supply the files.

Supplies – you will most certainly need supplies like paper, pens, folders and other small office equipment. Hole-punches, binding equipment, industrial staplers and filing cabinets are all considerations too. You will need to source an on-going supplier for things like paper (because you will use a lot of it) and set up an account with them. Make sure to compare the prices and credit terms for each supplier.

BUYING SOMEONE ELSE'S BUSINESS

Sometimes people find they do not like the business or they are not successful at it and want to get out. This can be a plus for you as they may have exactly what you need at a fraction of the cost.

So do your homework and ask a lot of questions. Why are you selling? How many existing clients do you have? Has the business been profitable for you, or not? If not, why not? Don't be afraid to ask, ask, and ask. The seller should be willing to provide you with almost anything that you want to know if they are being honest. Don't stop there either.

Make a list of what you would need this business to have to consider taking it over rather than starting your own. Compare the cost, convenience and structure of the business. Do you like what you see? Is the client list up to date and in good condition? Is the equipment in good condition?

If the existing business is in a separate office you will need to look at the premises and check that the lease can be transferred. Take the time to talk to other business owners in the area and absolutely contact some of their clients (with their permission, of course). Talk with the company's suppliers too. If everything seems legit and you want to move ahead, talk to a lawyer about it and find out what is needed to protect yourself from liability. The last thing you want to do is to take over someone else's mess.

YOUR BUSINESS AND THE LAW

Your first consideration should be deciding what form of a business you will use. Your business is a legal entity and the bookkeeping and tax considerations are different for each type. Most small businesses start out as sole proprietorships as they are the easiest and most cost effective to establish.

What form of business should I use?

Businesses can be a sole proprietorship, partnership, limited liability company (LLC), corporation, or an S corporation. Most small businesses start as a sole proprietorship as it is a business owned by a single individual. All you need is your space, equipment and education to start. There are no employees involved and minimal overhead. However, sole proprietorships do not limit your liability and your earnings and expenses are claimed with your other income, not separately.

If you decide to take on a partner, you will need to have legal documents drawn up describing your formal partnership agreement. This would include the divisions of labor, allocation of profits and other policies. Income and losses are divided according to the formal agreement and each partner claims on their own income tax return.

Corporations require a total separation of income and expenses from your personal finances. Corporations are more complex as they require more tax information and recordkeeping but they also offer you limited liability and tax benefits that are not available to other forms of business.

Lastly, there is the S corporation. S corporations do not pay any federal income taxes. Instead, the corporation's income or losses are divided among and passed through to its shareholders. The shareholders report the income or loss on their own individual income tax returns.

The legal part of a business is extremely important as it defines your relationship with the IRS and the limits of your liability should something go wrong. Consult a lawyer and find out the specifics for your particular business as there may be factors that you are not aware of. For example, most sole proprietorships operate under the owner's name. If you want to operate your business under a different name you may need a DBA (Doing Business As) or you may not. If you establish a corporation, your company name will need to be searched to ensure it is original and then registered. Make sure the legal details are clear – don't guess.

What kind of license do I need to operate a business?

Licensing requirements are very dependent on your location. Cities and states require different fees and registration processes. Contact your nearest Small Business Administration or Service Corps of Retired Executives (SCORE) for information. Both of these organizations offer free help when you are starting a business.

If you are hiring employees, you will need to apply for an Employer Identification Number (EIN) from the U.S. Internal Revenue Service. You will also need to set up a business bank account to separate your personal finances from your business books.

PROTECTING YOUR BUSINESS

Insurance is very important when you have a data entry business. Talk to your insurance broker about what kind of insurance coverage you need to protect you from burglary, fire, acts of God, theft, vandalism and liability. The amount invested in a comprehensive business policy is well worth it and it is a legitimate business expense as well.

If you live in a high risk area that is susceptible to tornados, hurricanes or earthquakes, make sure that your business is covered. Don't presume that you will be covered under your house policy because this may not be the case at all. Better to be safe than lose your business.

PROMOTING YOUR BUSINESS

Networking and professional connections

Having you own business requires networking and connecting with people, whether in your community, remotely, or both. This means that the development of networking skills is directly tied to the success or failure of your business. While 'networking' sounds like a complex and intimidating thing to do, many of the techniques are simple and painless:

LinkedIn – this is the business connection directory of the digital world. LinkedIn allows you to post your professional profile that describes what your background is, what your business does and ways to contact you and it's free.

Twitter – Twitter is a great application for sending out short messages to like-minded people in your network. Think of Twitter as the bulletin board to post what's new in 25 words or less. Twitter is also free.

Facebook –this platform has grown dramatically in recent years and many businesses have added pages to connect with their audience. Facebook's strongest feature is that you can add a personal touch to your business so people will know who you are and whether you are aligned with their business mindset. Facebook is free.

Forums – there are forums for just about everything on the internet and churches certainly have a presence there. This can be a good way to connect with someone within the church to find out what issues are important to them. Forums are free.

Professional Networks – join professional networks such as the International Virtual Assistants Association for a fee. This non-profit organization is dedicated to the professional education and development of members of the Virtual Assistance profession, and to educating the public on the role and function of the Virtual Assistant. Make sure you add your membership logo to your literature and website. You can also find free resources at Virtual Assistant Networking.

Website – it has never been easier to set up a website than it is today. Template website services such as Wordpress and Bluehost walk you through the process of building a simple website. All you have to do is design it and pay the monthly hosting fee.

Networking – is all about building friendships and getting business contacts. The more ways you find to reach out, the greater the likelihood of getting new clients.

MARKETING

Marketing is often confused with advertising. Advertising is buying print or online space to promote your business. Marketing is a plan that maps out how you want to promote your business, how much you want to spend and where. It has concrete goals and timelines so you can monitor your progress.

Once you have found where the churches are you will need to target the ones you want to reach. Clearly, with over 450,000 churches in the United States alone and only one of you, you would be hard-pressed to reach them all. Start closest to home and work outwards. Sort your list of churches from your Excel sheet by city and decide on your first contact.

If you have a lot of time, you can visit each church personally and try to talk to the minister or church secretary. Face to face introductions are still the best way to land new clients, but few people have the time to do this. Most rely on mail outs, flyers and advertising in small, local publications to start.

Creating marketing material can be a lot of fun and it doesn't have to be difficult. You will need to present your services to churches and put your best foot forward. This means you will need to have a nice flyer or personal letter describing your service. Once again, you can outsource the design work or try your hand at setting them up using readily available templates on the internet. Some business owners start by outsourcing the creation of a logo and then do the rest themselves. Make sure that material has been proofread and that there are no errors. Double check that all the contact information is correct such as email, website, telephone number and address.

You may also want to get business cards and stationery made, although a simple header in a word processing program will do for the latter until you get established. Business cards can be done by any online or local service. Services like Vistaprint and Gotprint will print cards for as little as $10 if you upload the design. They also have business accounts that offer discounts for business products and deliver right to your door free of charge. There are endless products that you can distribute for little money, such as pens, calendars, and notepads, that will put your name out there in the community. You do not need to stick to traditional methods. Unusual items may work in your favor but make a plan and a budget and stick to it.

One effective method of attracting new clients is to offer a free database setup to get them started. If a church has been thinking about this type of service, this may just be the push they need to get started. Other ideas include designing a special event flyer or newsletter at no charge or cleaning up their mailing list to show them how it should work.

Don't be discouraged if your marketing efforts don't produce an immediate response. It's rare that someone will have a need for your services at precisely the moment you contact them. Put together a professional information package and follow up on every one of them by telephone, letter or in-person. It's important that they keep you in mind, but don't plague clients with calls and letters or they will simply get fed up. Use your common sense and think about how often is reasonable.

Listing your business in the telephone directory is a good first step. As fewer and fewer people use an actual print book, make sure you claim your free Yellow Pages listing online. If you feel you want an added presence, you can upgrade to a featured advertisement which makes you easier to find in search engines. Be warned, these ads aren't cheap so plan wisely and incorporate them into your plan only when you can afford them.

ADVERTISING

Print advertisements and internet advertisements can be wonderful tools to attract new customers but once again you must know what you are doing. It is easy to drop a lot of money on advertising and see little or no return if it is not done correctly. Spend time to really target your market and then find publications that reach those markets. As a small business owner, small local publications that reach particular communities are less expensive and generally more effective for your needs. If you feel that you do not have the skills to figure out a marketing plan, outsource and hire a professional. You can have them work for you by the hour or for a set fee. Great sites for freelancers are Elance, ODesk and Guru. Make sure you read the guides they provide you with so you know how to post for optimum results.

Another way to advertise that is relatively inexpensive is by placing ads in the Christian newspaper classified section or even trying a small radio spot on a local station. Internet radio stations based out of your target area may have a large audience with very competitive rates. The creation of display ads and even creating audio files can all be outsourced for as little as $5 on sites like Fiverr. Heck, you can even get someone to dress up in a clown costume and sing about your company if that's what you want. The point is that you need to define who you want to reach, find the ways to reach them and set a defined budget to do it.

Marketing is also about measuring the success of your competitors and even emulating them at times. What works for them may work for you too. If the competition is too high in your area, try another area.

Referrals

Referrals are the backbone of any successful business and particularly with data entry as it requires a defined skill set and if done improperly it could lead to disaster for a church. Inaccurate or incomplete work could mean cash shortages, additional taxes and lost time to straighten everything out. If you are doing a good job and someone will vouch for you it's one big feather in your cap and you should wear it proudly. Referrals need not come from churches alone. Complementary businesses are also great sources for referrals. For example, print and copy shops often have customers who need word processing or desktop publishing done but they don't have the equipment, skills or staff to handle these services. This kind of work can give you that added income that you need when your data entry business is slow. Referrals are often a reciprocal agreement where you and other cooperating businesses refer clients to each other as the need arises.

Of course, many referrals are done simply because satisfied clients are happy with your work or from your friends and family. They may mention you to a church member who realizes that you have just what they are looking for.

Outside Resources

Information is the most important factor in determining whether you will be successful or not. Some small companies set up advisory boards of outside professional people to help them make educated decisions. These advisory boards can include an attorney, a certified public accountant, civic club leaders, owners or managers of businesses similar to yours, and retired executives. Members need only meet once a month and meetings focus on business problems and possible solutions.

Creating a Company Brochure

If you want to try to create a company brochure, Microsoft Word and Microsoft Publisher provide many colorful templates to create your own tri-fold brochure. Regardless of which one you choose, the instructions are basically the same:

Open the program and select "File", then "New" to create a new file.

Select the "Brochures & Booklets" tab, then the "Brochure" tab. Choose from one of the many templates that are available.

Add text and images to your brochure and play with the design. The entire template is filled with tips and tools to help you create an outstanding brochure even if you have never done it before. There are some clever ideas included in these tips that you may never have thought of on your own. You can easily personalize your brochure to fit your needs by deleting and adding your own text and images. When you like the look and feel of your brochure, save it with an appropriate name in a location that is easy to locate.

Print out your new Microsoft brochure and tweak it where necessary. Now that you have the file, you have the option of taking it to a print service that can produce it on high quality paper with a high resolution printer. These services will also fold your brochures for a fee as well.

If you feel all of this is just too much for you, hire someone to design it and then get someone to print it and fold it for you. The internet has made these types of services very accessible and affordable.

Examples of Brochure Copy

If you feel you can manage the design end of a brochure you still may not know what to put in an effective brochure. Here are some ideas of phrases that you can combine to create dynamic, effective copy for your brochure.

Example 1

ABC Data entry Service's church management solution supports your church's goals by centralizing your data into one easily accessible location. Our service embraces current technologies including social networking tools to help people connect, communicate, serve and build a community. Church members benefit from greater engagement and an improved sense of belonging. Your church benefits from robust insight into overall involvement, growth and impact.

Example 2

As a special bonus and thank you for signing up with ABC Data entry Service we will waive our normal data entry setup fee. This service has a regular value of $\$\_\_\_\_$ and we are offering it to you at no charge because we believe you will like what we do and will want to do more business with us.

Example 3

Is your church suffering due to the tough economic market? Are you looking for ways to maximize your revenues in new and creative ways? ABC Data entry Services can provide you with the up-to-date information you need to manage your ministry effectively and with vision. If you want detailed information on your congregation, ministry activities and financial accounts but you feel your resources are already stretched to their limit, consider ABC Data entry Services for creative solutions.

HOW TO FIND YOUR FIRST CLIENTS

Most Data entry professionals find their clients through word of mouth referrals, networking at church functions or advertising on the Internet. You might also try posting information about your service at online job boards, message boards, and home-business forums. Offline consider giving talks at local community centers about your service or posting ads in local newspapers.

FINDING A NICHE

It's a good idea to select one or more key market groups to target. There are a number of very valid reasons for choosing a well-defined market niche. By targeting a very specific market segment, you can tailor your brochure or flyer, reduce your costs and enjoy better results. A marketing plan is never written in stone. It should change as you learn and grow and by paying attention to who your clients are and what they want, you increase your chances of nabbing them as a client

INTRODUCTORY LETTERS TO CHURCHES

Sending out letters to churches in your area is likely the route you will choose for your first marketing effort. An effective marketing letter is like a resume. It must be short and to the point and it must explain why the potential client would even consider your services. Here are a few samples:

Example 1

Dear Church:

Modern technology could be saving your church a substantial amount of time and money. Are you still running your ministry in the same way it was ten, twenty or a hundred years ago? Most ministries don't have the time or the resources to maximize the data they have on their operations or they simply do not have enough information in the first place. ABC Data entry Services is your solution.

We are a locally owned and operated business that specializes in church data and church business. We will set up a system that is user-friendly, customizable and accessible anywhere at any time.

Example 2

ABC Data entry Services provides churches with a simple and easy system to help you track church membership information, contribution records, and much more. We offer tailored training to suit the needs of your church and can handle routine work at a fraction of the cost.

Example 3

I am sure you are always looking for different ways to improve the quality of service in your church while staying on budget. Database management, spreadsheets and data input are time consuming and take time away from other efforts. This type of work is easily outsourced and your data is always secure. The benefits to your church include readily accessible information, excellent reporting and higher productivity.

Example 4

My name is XXXXX from the ABC Data entry Services. My service is in the XXXXX area and it includes an extensive database for your church that will:

- Track membership information such as name, address, phone, email, date of birth, anniversaries, etc.

- Track contributions

- Transfers data into a mail merge program for letters and mailing

- Print reports on any conceivable combination of data that is available in the system including membership directories, staff lists, volunteer lists, special interest group lists and more.

Our work is 100% Satisfaction Guaranteed

Example 5

ABC Data entry Services provides an easy-to-use church management system that helps you to organize and manage your ministry. We include, free of charge, several directory database templates, a business directory, an employee directory, a member directory, and a personal directory.

Example 6

ABC Data entry Services is more than features and lists of people. It's a lens through which you will be able to observe and measure your impact on the community you serve. It's a powerful tool that should empower the people, systems and processes which support deeper engagement and life transformation.

Example 7

Dear Sir or Madam:

My name is XXXXX and I live in XXXXX. I run a secretarial business in XXXXX. I am writing this letter to you because I would like to offer my experience in data entry to your church. My experience comes from working in the secretarial and data entry field for the past XX years. For the past XX years, I worked for XXXXX in Microsoft Excel, PowerPoint, Microsoft Word and legal documentation. I have also worked for the XXXXX as a data entry professional.

I would like to offer my skills to help your office become better equipped to handle your data and fully automated for ease of use.

Example 8

Exactly what can our data entry service provide for your church?

When we create a database for you, it will give you access to all information you've added about your members in one place. Here, you'll find their photo, basic contact information and a list of groups that they participate in.

A database can be customized to set up a reminder to prompt for anniversaries, meetings, events or other items. It can also be programmed to send out letters for members who are grieving or if they have someone in the family who is ill. Having personalized information on your congregation gives you the ability to respond to each member personally and this creates a sense of belonging.

Advantages of a Remote Church Data Entry Service

There are many advantages to having someone handle your church database. Your secretary may be pressed for time and she cannot dedicate the time she would like to bring the database up to snuff or to design the forms necessary to record the data correctly from the start. Outsourcing data entry work means that you won't need extra computers or furniture and we are professionals, so we generally do a great job. Data entry can be repetitious and boring and many staff members simply don't want to do it. We do.

Here are some of the principle advantages of outsourcing your data entry work:

- Reduced expenses – no need to spend additional money on equipment, office space, software or training for something that most people don't even want to do.

- Accurate Billing – because we work remotely you only pay for the actual time that we spend on the job, not coffee breaks, lunch breaks and washroom breaks.

- Quick Turnaround – all we do is data so we are fast. We can input data quicker and more accurately than your in-house staff so the same work actually costs you less.

- Effective – we know this business and we do things right the first time around. This means there is little or no time spent 'tweaking' the original database as we consider your needs in the design.

- Organized – data management is a skill that is refined through experience. We know the best ways to organize your data so that it can produce the most useful reports.

- Optimized for Growth – we always set up your database with the big picture in mind. Your data will grow with your ministry and it will always be as relevant as it was when you started with our service.

Clearly, there are many more advantages but you know your services and your business. Think about what makes you unique and effective and put it in your letter.

WHAT ARE MY COMPANY`S RESPONSIBILITIES?

The data entered into the database belongs to the church and the church will have full access to it. Your job is to capture relevant data in an accurate manner and transfer into the database accurately and quickly.

As you are responsible for the accuracy of your work, you should establish system checks to review this work. These could include printing reports to spot obvious errors or having a second pair of eyes look at your work. Probably the most important way to ensure that the data is accurate is to create forms that reduce the possibility of errors.

While data entry will be your primary duty, you may also be asked to do a variety of other tasks. These could include sending letters and/or email messages to all or selected directory members, creating and printing a church directory or producing labels, reports, forms, letters, or brochures. The level of your involvement in administrative duties is totally up to you and the church.

You must also make sure that data is secure at home and at the church. One important aspect of database management is setting up a method of storing hard copies of various reports that is both secure, yet accessible to church staff. Important records should be stored in fire-proof containers and in a vault or safe when possible.

When you take on a new client make sure that you have a signed written contract in place that outlines your duties and fees. Your contract should include a clause limiting your liability. This is particularly true if you are a sole proprietor. This also avoids any discrepancies about billing, your credit policies and your responsibilities.

WHAT PRODUCTS CAN I PRODUCE?

Church Directory

A church directory is important and useful for a variety of reasons. First, a priest or pastor may use the directory to learn more about members and work towards ways of engaging them because of their interests.

Secondly, new church members can connect with existing members to find out about groups or events. Church directories also make it easier for members to put names to faces and remain connected. With planning and preparation, your church directory can be professional and effective and designed at a fraction of the cost.

Print Reports

Professional print reports can step thing up a notch so parishioners and business partners know that you are on top of your ministry. This can be particularly important during fundraising campaigns, grant proposals or any meeting that involves money. Who wants to give to a church that wastes money with poor administrative practices?

Mail Outs

Keeping in contact with members and visitors is vital to all churches. The most common way to do this is through newsletters or prayer letters. Many churches may not have the necessary staff to do all of the work involved and must rely on volunteers to help with getting letters ready to mail. Unfortunately, volunteers are not always available when you need them or they may not like this kind of work at all. Your service is fast, inexpensive and accurate.

Mailing Labels

Excel's extensive "filter," "sort" and "search" functions make it easy to create and manage a large contact database. You will be able to find and sort contacts by city, state, street, last name or any other criteria from the database you wish. Your contact list can be exported to Word and labels can be setup to print in any size or quantity.

Business Directory

Creating a business directory of members is a good way to support businesses that have practices in line with the church. Business directories can help the congregation to find a business and support them by using their services. This, in turn, may help the church by way of donations of goods or services.

A professional business directory is a good source of revenue for the church too as they can sell advertising space to local businesses.

Other Products

ID Cards with photos, if required
Volunteer Lists
Special Interest Group Lists
Employee Lists
Telephone Lists
Payroll Reports
Taxation Documents
Emails & Email Campaigns

WHAT SERVICES SHOULD I OFFER?

You can offer a wide range of services. The following list covers what we found on the market, but it is by no means complete. Some of these services could be businesses on their own while others are great supplementary activities to your data entry work. Your clients will tell you what they want and then it's up to you to supply it.

Transcription

People on the go rarely have time to sit down and type a letter. In a church environment, this is particularly true. An excellent additional service to data entry is transcription. Transcription is simply turning audio files into written documents. While there are different types of transcriptions, most often you will find that church transcriptions are either conversations between a few people in a meeting or an audio recording of a meeting of some kind. Occasionally, a minister may record a telephone conversation to have a record of important information.

If you know how to type, you can provide transcription services for business owners and entrepreneurs from your own home. You don't need any specialized training. You just need typing skills, transcription software and a specialized pedal to start, stop and rewind the recording. Even the pedal is optional, but it does make the job go a lot quicker. Of course, accuracy is important and if you want to make a decent amount of money doing it you need to be fast too. After typing the dictated information, the typist sends the typed text file back to the employer.

Who needs transcription services? Transcription is quickly becoming one of the most used methods of recording information. Few secretaries know shorthand today and voice recordings have the added advantage of being able to be replayed if a word or phrase is missed. Public speakers and workshop or seminar leaders often transcribe their seminars and talks. Ministers may dictate letters, memos or to do lists to keep them on top of their work. Transcription is certainly not limited to church work. It is used in most industries and that is why the work is abundant.

Transcribe Via the Internet

The lion's share of transcription work is done via the internet today. Clients send an MP3 audio recording which you play through transcription software. This software allows you to control the play and stop functions of the recording.

The goal of transcription is to do it as fast and as accurately as possible in order to make the most money. A foot pedal and headphones are a good investment as recordings are not always as clear as one might like them to be. Free transcription software, such as Express Scribe, (NCH Software) is available for download on the internet for free.

One of the best ways to get your foot in the door at a church is contract your services for transcription of church services and meetings. We live in a digital world and pastors and ministers often post their sermons on their website blogs too. Many other like a transcription as their sermon is not always delivered in the manner that they planned.

There are several ways to send files. Normally, email is the easiest. However, large audio files are often exceeds email file size restrictions and other means must be set up. There are free cloud services, such as Dropbox, (https://www.dropbox.com) that provide virtually unlimited storage for files. You and your client 'share' a file folder and you can drop and remove files as needed. It really couldn't be simpler.

Letter Service for the Church

Writing letters for the church is a wonderful service to offer pastors and church staff to help them keep in touch with members of the congregation, and to reach out to those in the community. There are letters for just about every occasion but a church rarely has the staff to prepare them and send them. Your business can provide this service and it is so easy to set up.

Use Word to design a template and save it. Each time the church needs the letter all you have to do is drop in the recipients' details, print a mailing label and put it in an envelope. Church letters must always express sincerity and offer the assistance and support of the church. They may also end with an appropriate quote suitable to the topic. Here are some of the major categories of letters but this is by no means all of them:

Attendance
Bible School
Church Financials
Church Policies
Congratulations
Counseling
Deacons – Elders
Employment
Facilities
Finances - Member
Fundraising
Funeral
Guest Speaker
Honorarium
Illness or Accident
Incarcerated Member
Invitations
Meetings
Revivals
Military Member
Outreach – Invite to Church
Outreach – Invite To Event
Outreach – Thank You
Outreach – Welcome
Outside Speaking Engagement
Personnel
Retreats
Seminars
Special Events
Missionary
Volunteers

Mailing Service

An additional service to offer your clients is a mailing service. Good organizational skills, a postage meter and a desktop computer and printer are about all you need to get this business going. A mailing service is ideal for churches as they often do large newsletter mailings and fundraising campaigns throughout the year. Holidays are especially busy times for churches and also one of their best times for raising funds. Letter to businesses, members, and communities are often many at this time of the year.

Setting up Your First Database

A church database will provide basic information about every member of the congregation, every visitor and every employee. A database ensures that everything stays organized, current, and accessible within the organization.

First, you will need to collect contact information from everyone who attends the church. Ask the church pastor to make an announcement that the church will be creating a roster with contact information. Request that all members pick up an information sheet, fill it out and return it to you. Place this announcement in the church bulletin for at least a month prior to the deadline for return of the information sheets. If you have email addresses for members, you can send an email with a form attached that they can fill out online.

In order to create a database with few mistakes, you should use consistent fields. Here is a format you may wish to use when creating your form:

Mr. Mrs. Ms. / Fname / Lname / Suffix / Title-Attention Line / Address1 / Address2 / City / State / Zip / Phone # / Mobil # / Fax / Email / Anniversary / Birthday / Member (active/inactive) / Visitor / Group1 / Group2 / Volunteer / photo / Publish? Y/N / Company / Face book / Category /Notes

There are some address-correcting programs that will check each address against the national postal database and verify that it matches what is in the postal database. Use www.addressdoctor.com or www.smartsoftusa.com to confirm that the address is correct. Members should always have the choice to opt out of public directories if they wish as indicated by the 'Publish Y/N' field.

SETTING YOUR FEES

Setting your fees may well be one of the most difficult parts of establishing a successful business. If you price your products too low you will not earn enough profit to cover your expenses, plan for the future and earn some decent money. If you price too high you can price yourself out of work and the competition will pick up the business instead of you. While there is no set way to set your prices there are some helpful guidelines to follow.

The simplest method for establishing your prices is to call around, check the internet and talk to people in your area about the particular services you offer. Others decide what they want as their net income and work backwards to figure out how much to charge to reach this number. Yet others price per job and have a set price per page or per hour.

Probably the most intelligent solution is a combined approach that considers the skill level of the particular project, your profit goals and the market. You need to set up a system that provides a structure so you can quote consistent, fair rates.

Hourly Rate

Charging by the hour is common for word processing work, however you should set up a rate scale that is based on the complexity and skill level required. Clearly some work will be more difficult than others.

An example would be that your hourly rate ranges from $28 for straight word processing up to $40 for complex desktop publishing. Sources suggest you consider using levels like these to rate the work complexity and skill level needed:

Level 1

(lowest hourly rate)

Basic word processing, routine clerical services, simple proofreading

Level 2

Enhanced word processing, copyediting, proofreading, basic spreadsheet design, internet research

Level 3

Desktop publishing, spreadsheet design, simple web page design, simple web page maintenance

Level 4

Graphic design, writing (academic, business, resume, technical), web page design, web page maintenance

Level 5

(highest hourly rate)

Consulting, training

If a job requires multiple skills, then adjust your rate accordingly. Many jobs may fall in between the rates you have set and that should not be an issue as long as you record how much you charged for a combination of work. You do not want to be caught charging a different amount for the same work in the future unless it is due to a rate increase. Keep refining your price list until it is more and more specific. This list is for your reference only.

Provide each client with a quote (written or verbal) so there is never any misunderstanding about what they will be billed. This is helpful to you too as you can take notes and track how long the work actually took and measure the complexity so you can improve your future bids. In many ways, pricing is set by trial and error. Be sure to let a client know if you think the job is going to exceed your estimate and why. No client wants to feel that they have been deceived and it is better to be upfront with them so they can decide if they want to continue.

Many businesses use a quotation form for all jobs that is easy to reference. Most accounting software programs allow you to issue a quote and switch it to an invoice with the click of the mouse which makes billing a breeze. A recent survey of business support services found that the hourly rate ranges for the most popular services offered by respondents were:

Basic word processing $12-40
Enhanced word processing $15-50
Copyediting $17-75
Database entry $18-50
Transcription, general $15-45
Consulting/training $17-90
Spreadsheet design $15-75
Desktop publishing $17-75
Graphic design $14-100
Website design $20-150
Internet research $17-75

Job Estimates

Estimating jobs requires a system that you use each time you want to price a job. First, determine an appropriate hourly rate. Second, estimate how long you think the job will take. Obviously, you will get better at this as time goes on and your clients will be the first to tell you that your bid is too high, but they will never say a word when you are below the market rate. If the estimated hours for the job are multiplied by the rate and it feels too low to you, it likely is.

Factors Affecting Data Entry Costs

Most data entry work is calculated using a cost-based approach. Calculate how much your time is worth and then add a percentage for overhead and profit. Once again, your pricing structure will be defined over time. This is the primary reason for the quotation process as it allows you to adjust as you see fit.

Most data entry projects will fall in the range of 15 cents to 50 cents per data record. However, this is just a general estimate and fees can sometimes be much higher of lower. When describing a 'record' one means all the fields identified by the client as representing a complete, identifiable (and billable) string of information. Most times this is a row in a spreadsheet. Other times, a 'record' may be all the information on an entire form, such as registration form.

One other factor will affect fee is the size of the project. Ongoing projects must be priced aggressively to reflect the volume of the work. Remember, this is steady money that is coming into business and you do not have marketing or advertising costs associated with it. Try to achieve a gross margin ranging from 30% for very large projects (hundreds of records), to 45% for smaller, one-time projects.

Every project is unique, and each client has different goals and objectives. Here are some considerations when pricing your work.

Document Intake

Preparing documents for data entry can be simple or complex and time consuming. It is important that your time be estimated accordingly. Document intake includes removing staples, paper clips, and post-it notes, and arranging all of the documents right-side-up and facing the same direction prior to scanning. Folded pages must be unfolded and aligned with stack.

Some clients will prepare the documents before they deliver them to avoid additional costs but it naturally increases the amount of time and effort they must spend on the documents and can slow down the turnaround time on the work as they are rarely as adept. The cost of document preparation usually exceeds the actual cost of scanning. Scanning costs can range from 2.5 cents to 10 cents per document, depending on the factors below.

Document Scanning

Most data entry starts when the client delivers actual paper documents into your hands. You prepare the document as described above and then scan each sheet of paper. There are many factors that can affect scanning costs including:

Document Size – documents can be in non-standard sizes. Those that are too big for the scanning bed must be done in sections and those that are too small require additional attention to alignment and often enlargement too.

Document Uniformity – clients may send a group of documents that have varying page sizes.

Paper Type – the source paper may be thin and fragile or there may be stickers attached.

Document Condition - some pages may be faded or on colored paper and the scan will require enhancement which takes extra time.

Batch Integrity - Can you scan continuously, or do you have to retain client batch integrity?

Document Complexity

Size – how many pages does the document have?
Fields – how many unique fields are on each page?
Records – how many records are on each page?

Editing

Some data must be manipulated to be useful. This includes integrating client-provided lookup tables, making address corrections, or standardizing the format of the data provided.

Output File

Does the client want the results in a report or simply as raw data? Do they want the data sorted into groups and then dropped into a publication?

Data Entry

How many fields need to be keyed?

How many characters are in each field?

What type of data is it? Is it strictly numeric, strictly alpha or a combination of the two?

Form Design

If the form the data is on is poorly designed it will have a huge impact on data entry efficiency and cost. If this is the case, you may suggest to the client that you could design a better form to reduce their costs (and to make your life a lot easier).

'Constrained' forms only allow each person to write one letter or number in each 'box' on the form. This improves legibility and reduces the chances of input errors.

Legibility

Are the documents handwritten or typed? Is the data consistent throughout the document?

EFFECTIVE DATA ENTRY

Accuracy is the most important factor in data entry. Single-key data entry should be between 95 and 97% accurate, depending on the type of data. The more complex the data is, the higher the likelihood there will be errors.

You will be the most effective at this work when you are the most experienced and this is the primary motivator if you decide to hire too. A data entry clerk may be fast but it is the knowledge of how to handle particular situations that make them valuable to you. Naturally, a combination of both is preferable. Make sure your employees have excellent English language skills so that they can spot obvious errors and correct these errors as they work.

DATA ENTRY TURNAROUND TIME

The general rule of thumb is the faster the required turnaround time, the higher the fee. This is to compensate for having to work staff longer and harder during short periods of time, as well as the added administrative burden to get a job done quickly.

For large, ongoing projects you can allot hours in a systematic manner so the work gets done on time and on budget. Work like this is often done within set guidelines for receiving source documents and submitting processed data. You may be able to transmit completed work daily.

Typical turnaround times range from 48 hours to one-week. However, time-sensitive projects may require a turnaround time of as little as 3 hours.

QUALITY IN FORMS PROCESSING

Field Validation

You can customize particular fields to validate your input to reduce the possibility of errors. Common field validations include city names, state names, zip codes with lookups from postal code tables and customer specific data, such as members' names, program names or contribution lists.

Re-Key Verification

When accuracy is paramount, selected fields can be re-keyed. Once the data has been input a second operator keys the information in again and the results are compared to spot errors.

Address Correction & Verification

Undeliverable mail is very costly to organizations undertaking large direct mail programs. To reduce this cost make sure all data adheres to USPS standards.

Data Layout

The most effective way to promote legible handwriting is to only allow one letter or number in each block of the data input form.

Whether you are keying data from paper, a scanned image, or using recognition technology, a constrained form will vastly improve the chances of data entry accuracy and efficiency.

Number Each Field or Question

When you have a complex, multi-page questionnaire or survey involving many different fields and many different types of fields you should always number each question. This reduces the possibility for error and makes data review more effective.

Match Forms to Spreadsheets

Each new spreadsheet should reflect the fields that exist in the original form in the same order so that keying is quick and accurate. Reversing columns or changing the titles is not recommended. Fast data entry involves conformity and the less that needs to be read, the faster and more accurate the data entry will be.

Use Check Boxes

When possible, use check boxes to standardize answers and promote single-value entries. Check boxes may not be a good solution when dealing with complex forms involving hundreds of answers as the data entry operator has to match up the response on the form to the corresponding field on the data entry screen.

Use Reasonable Field Sizes

Make sure that your field size is large enough to accommodate the longest data. Too often, we see forms too small and the person filling in the information does not have enough blocks to print the information. An example of this is often seen when a business wants to record an email address. The average e-mail address is 20 characters long, yet you should allow room for at least 30-35 characters. The average name, including middle initial, is 15 characters, the average address is 16 characters, and the average city is 12. However, an average is just that, an average. It is better to have too many blocks than not enough.

OTHER BUSINESS SUPPORT SERVICES

Let other existing business owners know you're available for overflow or to work on a contract basis. You may have to sign confidentiality and non-competing agreements and take a lower rate too. However, this business will come to you without you having to chase after it so you will have no marketing or advertising costs. These services may include:

Word processing
Desktop publishing
Spreadsheet design
College papers and reports
Telephone answering
Mail receiving and forwarding
Packing and shipping
Database/mailing list management
Bookkeeping, check preparation and invoicing
Resume preparation
Proofreading
Print brokering
Photocopying
Notary
Internet research
Web page design and maintenance
Event planning
Consulting
Training

If you have experience in a specific field, target it for extra work. Two of the most common of these are legal and medical transcription as they have very specific terminology and formatting requirements.

Another group that can add on to your business includes others that work from home too. While they are normally specialists in their own field, they can't do everything and you might be able to do what they cannot.

If your business is near a college or university you can promote your business for students, instructors and even busy administrators. Word travels fast when you are good at what you do and there are plenty of students in institutions.

BUSINESS PLAN

A business plan is guidance, an important assistant for anyone who starts or runs a business. Business plans take some time to write, but in the long term, you may save much time and cash flow. Get some of the information you need here.

You may need a business plan to apply for bank loans or getting investors for financial support. Here is some help with writing your business plan:

1.0 Executive Summary

ABC Data Entry Service is a new start up data entry business. The company is a sole proprietorship with Jane Doe as the founder and sole employee. The company was formed and will serve a variable geographic customer segment.

The Market

ABC Data Entry Service has identified three distinct market segments which will be targeted. The first segment is churches. These organizations, in large part due to their status as a not for profit do not have excess capital. As a consequence, they have tried to maximize office staff's tasks and responsibilities as much as possible. This means most employees are quite busy. When a random data entry task comes up the church typically does not have an employee that can handle the task. This is good for ABC Data Entry Service who can quickly and seamlessly take over tasks. This saves the church money because they are only paying for the labor needed to complete the task.

The second customer segment is individuals. This is an attractive segment because as our daily lives become busier and busier we have less and less free time. Using ABC Data Entry Service is one way to create more free time, or at least not have to do tasks that we may not prefer to. It is anticipated that the services provided to individuals will be more menial relative to the services provided to companies.

The last customer segment is companies of various sizes. In the current business climate, there has been a common occurrence to have wide scale corporate downsizing. This is helpful for ABC Data Entry Service because the downsizing means that people kept within the company are busier than ever. Typically in a downsizing climate there is the outsourcing of projects/jobs that the current staff cannot handle. ABC Data Entry Service believes that a portion of their sales (relative to the other customer segments) will come from companies.

Services

ABC Data Entry Service offers a wide range of services. The bulk of the services are data entry, mailing list updates, etc. These will be the services that will be billed out at the lower end of the billing spectrum of $25-$45. Services that are billed out near the top of the range are those that require higher levels of skills such as accounting, marketing, and graphic design. In the middle will be services such as word processing which in themselves is a wide range of services. The offered services will be things that the customer does not have time for or things that they choose not to do, and would prefer someone else to take care.

Competitive Edge

The majority of ABC Data Entry Service Services are data entry in nature. They are jobs that most administrative assistants can't handle. ABC Data Entry Service will be using their competitive edge of a wide range of skills to their fullest. In addition to the more menial tasks, ABC Data Entry Service is also able to offer clients a wide range of more technical skills such as proficiency with QuickBooks Pro for accounting issues, graphic design with skill in both Photoshop and PageMaker, and well-honed marketing and research skills. This is a competitive edge because once a client has found a data entry specialist they have an economic incentive to continue to use them as opposed to finding someone else (assuming that they are happy with the level of service and the work product). The problem occurs when the client is happy with the data entry specialist but needs work on a project that the specialist does not have skills in, consequently, the client must look elsewhere. An advantage is created when the specialist (ABC Data Entry Service) has a wider and more complex range of skills, they are then able to offer more value to the client.

ABC Data Entry Service is an exciting application of the data entry business model, providing a wide range of customer services from a local and remote location, leveraging the power of the Internet and home office. This is a very efficient business model and will provide Jane with reasonable income and the flexibility to handle the jobs when and how she chooses. The sales forecast indicates revenue will rise for year two and year three along with corresponding net profit increases.

1.1 Keys to Success

- Offer a wide range of services allowing ABC Data Entry Service to handle any type of task.

- • Maintain a flexible enough schedule so last minute projects can be completed.

- • Ensure accurate billing and project estimates.

1.2 Mission

ABC Data Entry Service's mission is to offer the highest level of administrative assistant services as well as an expertise in data entry. ABC Data Entry Service will be able to handle a wide range of tasks with a level of professionalism and trust that is hard to come by in today's world. ABC Data Entry Service will exceed customer's expectations.

1.3 Objectives

- To generate over $35,000 in the first year.

- To develop enough income to make the job full time position.

- To be able to decrease the marketing expenses after a couple of years because there are sufficient word of mouth projects to remain busy.

2.0 Company Summary

ABC Data Entry Service has been formed as a sole proprietorship by Jane Doe. The company will incur some start expenses detailed in section 2.2.

2.1 Company Ownership

Jane Doe has formed ABC Data Entry Service as a sole proprietorship. Jane will invest money of her own as well as money received from her family.

2.2 Start-up Summary

The following equipment/services will be needed for purchase to allow ABC Data Entry Service to begin operations:

- Microsoft windows •

- Computer

- Laser printer

- Internet connection

- Scanner

- Fax machine

- Copier

- Various software including adobe acrobat, photoshop and pagemaker, Microsoft office, word, and QuickBooks pro

- A standard contract template for clients

Table:

Start-up
Start-up Requirements
Start-up Expenses
Legal $
Website Development $
Insurance $
Rent $
Total Start-up Expenses $
Start-up Assets
Cash Required $
Other Current Assets $
Long-term Assets $
Total Assets $
Total Requirements $

Table:

Start-up Funding

Start-up Expenses to Fund $

Start-up Assets to Fund $

Total Funding Required $

Assets Non-cash Assets from Start-up $

Cash Requirements from Start-up $

Additional Cash Raised $

Cash Balance on Starting Date $

Total Assets $

Liabilities and Capital

Liabilities Current Borrowing $

Long-term Liabilities $

Accounts Payable (Outstanding Bills) $

Other Current Liabilities (interest-free) $

Total Liabilities $

Capital Planned Investment Jane $

Family $

Additional Investment Requirement $

Total Planned Investment $

Loss at Start-up (Start-up Expenses) ($)

Total Capital $

Total Capital and Liabilities $

Total Funding $

3.0 Services

ABC Data Entry Service provides a wide range of data entry and secretarial functions from a local and remote location. ABC Data Entry Service will serve a wide range of clients from businesses to individuals to not-for-profit organizations. The following is a list (not exhaustive) of the different services offered. Please note that as long as Jane has the skills to complete a task, she will be willing to undertake whatever project the client may wish:

- Data entry

- Word processing

- Accounting/bookkeeping

- Marketing

- Billing

- Desktop publishing

- Travel arrangements

- Mailing services

- Research

- Maintain electronic mailing lists

- Maintain vendor files

- Concierge services

ABC Data Entry Service has the ability to provide any needed service for a client. Some of the services will be tasks that the client does not have time or staff for. Other tasks may be things that the client just does not have the desire to do. Either way, ABC Data Entry Service will offer a service to seamlessly assist clients with a wide range of tasks.

This is of considerable value to the customer. The client incurs no payroll taxes, no insurance costs as well as no fringe benefit expenses. The client is not responsible for providing office space or equipment. This is contained in ABC Data Entry Service hourly rate. The hourly rate is $25-$45 depending on the activity. More menial tasks such as data entry will be billed out at $25, activities such as graphic design, accounting, and other more skilled tasks will be billed out at $45.

ABC Data Entry Service will be operating out of Jane's home. A room has been dedicated to the business in the house and rent will be paid for the use of the room.

4.0 Market Analysis Summary

ABC Data Entry Service has segmented the market into three attractive, distinct, customer segments. Services will target churches, companies, individuals, and not for profit organizations. Market research indicates that these are the most likely consumers of data entry specialists. The data entry business for churches is fairly new, proliferating with the Internet which allows service providers in remote locations to serve a large geographic range of clients. Membership records within the larger data entry associations indicate that there are typically one data entry specialist within each state.

4.1 Market Segmentation

ABC Data Entry Service has identified three customer segments which are the most attractive for the data entry industry. These segments are customers who tend to consume the largest amount of data entry services.

Churches

These organizations are attractive customers because they are often in a funding crunch. They often do not have the funding to have some sort of assistant always on staff ready to do work as it comes along. The not-for-profit organizations are often as trim as possible regarding staffing. This sets up an excellent opportunity for ABC Data Entry Service who can provide administrative services when needed, but are not a resource drain when there is no work. ABC Data Entry Service will serve a wide range of not-for-profit churches.

Companies

For a variety of reasons companies are an attractive segment. Some companies have been going through corporate downsizing as a means for decreasing overhead. While this does assist reducing monthly expenditures, often the company soon thereafter realizes that were certain necessary services being provided by the personnel that were let go. Companies also use data entry specialists for projects that come up with little notice and they need a helping hand. The data entry specialist is particularly useful because the companies only pay for the services rendered; there is no continual employment or equipment overhead.

There are 36,554 potential customers · Sizes for companies range from small organizations of a few people to large corporations · some companies will use ABC Data Entry Service on a random basis; others may sign ABC Data Entry Service initially on a retainer basis. This arrangement is initial because once business become fuller, the highest billing rate work will be sought out since the number of hours available is limited.

Individuals

Data entry specialists are also useful to many different individuals. The individuals are likely to use the assistants for tasks that they do not have time for or tasks that they simply do not enjoy. These tasks could be business related, but research indicates that many of the requested tasks are personal in nature, assisting the individual with something that they do not have time for. One unexpected tasks is trip planning. The client provides the assistant with some guidelines and the assistant performs a comprehensive search of options as well as discounts/ specials.

Typically ages 30-67 · Median individual income is $51,000 · 91% of the individuals have a college degree · 32% have a graduate degree.

4.2 Target Market Segment Strategy

The targeted customers: churches, companies, and individuals, were chosen because they all are likely to have a need for a data entry specialist, all for different reasons. As companies continue to become as efficient as possible, they are keeping their current employees as busy as possible. Often they are too busy to take care of projects that come up randomly, that is where ABC Data Entry Service comes in.

Individuals will have a demand for ABC Data Entry Service for tasks that they either do not have the time for or do not want to do. This is especially true as we (Americans) have less and less free time. This then fuels our desire to pick and choose the activities that we have time for or care to do, and then subcontract out the things we do not do. Churches are also attractive as they are the organizations who often have the least funds so creative options to complete tasks are always considered. ABC Data Entry Service allows them to have someone complete the task without the typical overhead associated with the worker.

4.3 Service Business Analysis

Data entry specialist is a fairly new industry that has arisen from the convenience of the Internet. The Internet created a medium where people could communicate, transfer files electronically, do research, and find people all from one's home. In essence the Internet has created a "web" connecting people in remote locations.

The other factor that fueled the growth of data entry specialist was the downsizing of the business world. This created a lot of opportunities for data entry specialist because companies were getting slimmer and slimmer and for the small, random projects that would pop up they would just subcontract out the work. When you combine the market need for projects and the Internet as the connection to these remote people, you have a new business model.

There has also been the development of a few organizations that specifically serve data entry specialist that has assisted the growth and legitimacy of the industry. The associations have developed certification programs that have assisted growth by helping establish trust between two unknown parties. The certifications provide indications of minimum levels of skills as well as work product.

As technology increases, more and more tasks will be able to be accomplished remotely, sending the finished product electronically as well as even having face to face video conferences remotely allowing simulating a face to face meeting, however, the two parties could be half way around the world.

4.3.1 Competition and Buying Patterns

By virtue of the nature of data entry specialist, competition does not have a significant physical boundary. While there typically are 1-5 registered/data entry specialist per state, there is no advantage in choosing a data entry specialist from one state relative to another state. Data entry specialists therefore compete on availability, costs, work product and skill set.

If the projects are easy, costs is likely going to be a main choice factor. If time is of the essence then availability will rule, lastly if the task is difficult the data entry specialist is likely to be chosen on their ability to handle the task. Please note that these considerations are primarily for the initial selection of a data entry specialist. Once a DEA has been found and has been used a couple of times, it is likely that the client will not be looking for a new DEA but will maintain a working relationship with the existing DEA, assuming of course that the client's satisfaction is maintained.

5.0 Strategy and Implementation Summary

ABC Data Entry Service will leverage their competitive edge of having a wide range of services offered. This will be especially useful since once a client has found a DEA that they are happy with they will tend to continue to use them assuming the DEA can handle all of the tasks that the client has.

ABC Data Entry Service marketing strategy will develop visibility and awareness for the company as a data entry specialist. This will be accomplished by using several marketing mediums. Lastly, ABC Data Entry Service will highlight in their sales strategy the high level of customer satisfaction that ABC Data Entry Service offers. This is especially important since repeat business from a customer is likely if they are kept happy.

5.1 Competitive Edge

ABC Data Entry Service's competitive edge is the wide range of skills that they offer to clients. While many of the DEA's can offer basic administrative skills and tasks, ABC Data Entry Service has an expanded selection of skills that includes accounting/bookkeeping, graphic design, and marketing.

Having the wider range of skills is significant because the nature of the industry is that once a good service provider is found the client tends to use the DEA for all of the needs the DEA can fill. If there are tasks that the DEA cannot do the client will look elsewhere to have those tasks completed. Here in lays the danger, the possibility that the client will find a new DEA, one that is more diverse and stay with the new DEA. By offering a wide range of services ABC Data Entry Service can be the one stop DEA serving all of the client's needs.

5.2 Marketing Strategy

ABC Data Entry Service's marketing strategy will seek to raise awareness of ABC Data Entry Service as a premier DEA. The first method that they will use is membership to the Data Entry Management Association (DEMA). This association offers a certification process which is useful when you are trying to sell the services over the Internet and the prospective customer does not know you.

The certification develops some degree of trust because the certification provides an indication of professionalism, acceptable work products, and appropriate skills. This will tend to speed up the process of developing trust between ABC Data Entry Service and the remote client. Being a member of the association is also useful because it includes ABC Data Entry Service in their DEMA directory. This comes into play when clients are looking for a DEA and they will often visit an association's website looking for a DEA and they will see ABC Data Entry Service

ABC Data Entry Service will also have a website developed that will be a showcase for the services that they offer. This must be a professional site because other than phone conversations, this is the impression that is initially left on the client, the more professional the site looks, the better the image that is bestowed on ABC Data Entry Service

ABC Data Entry Service will also place some advertisements in a couple newspapers. The choice of newspaper will be based on several factors:

- Low cost, high readership

- In a region that has had significant corporate downsizing

- A concentrated urban area

The effectiveness of a newspaper advertisement is somewhat unknown. The ads will be run a few times and a costs benefit analysis will be done to decide future use.

5.3 Sales Strategy

The sales strategy will be based on ensuring complete customer satisfaction. This will be addressed because the chance of repeat business is very high. This is intuitive because once you have found a data entry specialist and have used them for a while a trust relationship builds where you begin to feel more and more comfortable with this new person.

There then is a decreased chance of looking for a different DEA as the switching costs increase because of the time it takes to find someone new and build trust. ABC Data Entry Service will be successful in developing superior customer satisfaction so that the majority of their clients will become repeat clients. As more and more business is repeat business, marketing costs fall because with a one person business, there is a finite amount of business that ABC Data Entry Service can handle in a month.

The more business that is received through repeat business, the less business ABC Data Entry Service will have to market themselves. Additionally, the more business that comes to ABC Data Entry Service the more selective they can be (assuming they are reaching full capacity) in choosing the projects. Projects with higher billing can be chosen increasing revenue for the same amount of hours worked.

The key to customer satisfaction is ensuring that all customers are more than happy. If it turns out of the customers is not happy with the project it is worthwhile to correct the situation, even if it is costly in the short run. In the long term, the customer should be convinced to remain with ABC Data Entry Service and is even likely to tell others about how ABC Data Entry Service went out of their way to correct the problem. This develops incredible good will. Even if services have to be given away to ensure complete satisfaction that short term cost will is a worthwhile investment for the long term sustainability of the business.

5.3.1 Sales Forecast

A sales forecast has been developed to measure the sales by month for the first year and yearly for years two and three. The sales forecast has been used to help predict the Break-even Point by measuring revenue against expenses.

A conservative forecast has been adopted to increase the chance of meeting the sales goals. The sales have been broken down by the specific customers as a method of tracking where the business is coming from. The following charts and graphs provide quantifiable data and graphic representations of the sales.

Table: Sales Forecast

5.4 Milestones

ABC Data Entry Service has chosen several different quantifiable milestones for the company. Milestones are being used as a method of setting goals as well as then tracking progress toward the attainment of the goals. The following goals have been chosen:

- Business plan completion

- First customer

- Profitability

- Full time employment

- Decreased marketing costs

Please review the following table for more detail regarding the milestones.

Table: Milestones

6.0 Web Plan Summary

A website will be developed and used as a marketing tool to put a "face" on ABC Data Entry Service By virtue of the type of company that ABC Data Entry Service is, the only interaction or visibility that ABC Data Entry Service will have with clients is personal visitation and conversation over the phone, an exchange of work product, as well as viewing the website.

The website will be developed to provide information about ABC Data Entry Service and the services that they offer. In addition to providing information, the website will serve as a way of creating an image or facade of ABC Data Entry Service to customers who are in remote locations. Said another way, the more professional that the website is, the more professionalism that is exuded toward ABC Data Entry Service For many the website will be the first impression of ABC Data Entry Service As we all know first impressions can be quite important so ABC Data Entry Service has decided to invest money into the site to ensure a professional looking site.

6.1 Website Marketing Strategy

The website will be primarily marketed through the following methods:

- Search engine submission. When someone is interested in finding a data entry specialist they will often type "data entry" into a search engine such as Google! And they will receive a list of sites that have relevance to the key word. ABC Data Entry Service will submit their site and applicable key words to various search engines to ensure that they are high on the list of results.

- URL on all printed material. For advertisements in the newspaper or any correspondence from ABC Data Entry Service, the website will be listed on the printed material encouraging people to visit the site and find more information.

- Association membership. One of the values of being a member of a DE association is being included in their directory of service provider websites. Some people will go right to the association's web page to research various DEAs. In this case they will find links to ABC Data Entry Service site.

6.2 Development Requirements

The site will be professionally developed for the cost of $5,000.

7.0 Management Summary

Jane Doe received her undergraduate degree in business administration from the University of XYZ. Upon graduation Jane went to work for the XYZ Corporation supporting their marketing department. While her position had the majority of responsibilities as an administrative assistant, she was cross trained in a variety of areas including some graphic design, data entry, accounting and marketing.

This was fairly unusual for XYZ which typically has narrow job descriptions for their employees. However, in the marketing department, it was smaller, closer knit group of people so when the group needed something done they would often have it accomplished by someone within the group. If the person did not know the skill but there was someone in the group that did, they would often train the other person which would in effect increase the flexibility of the department. It was the time spent in this department that Jane developed her large repertoire of skills.

Upon entering back into the working world, Jane began to realize that jobs were more difficult to come by. At the same time Jane began considering a nontraditional job that would give her more flexibility to spend with her family. A friend of hers was telling her about an acquaintance of theirs who started her own DEA company. This intrigued Jane, she had the skills to pull it off, it just made her a bit nervous to start her own business, and the process seamed overwhelming.

At this point Jane had to decide something so she began to write a business plan and then make the decision as to whether to continue with the DEA idea or to find something else. When she was working on the business plan, she was forced to consider and make decisions regarding a wide range of topics that affect a business; she began to feel more comfortable about starting her own business. The writing of the plan forced her to conceptualize a lot of topics and she quickly realized that starting a business was well within her ability. The plan was completed, and she started operations.

7.1 Personnel Plan

Jane will be the sole employee. While the business could generate more revenue if she hired and trained additional people, her need for reasonable income, flexibility, enjoyable work, and full time employment was satiated so it will remain a one person business. Jane will be taking a base salary with the expectation that she will also be able to use some of the net profit once it starts accumulating.

Table:

Personnel

8.0 Financial Plan

The following sections will outline important financial information.

8.1 Important Assumptions

The following table details important Financial Assumptions.

Table: General Assumptions

8.2 Break-even Analysis

The Break-even Analysis indicates what will be needed in monthly revenue to reach the breakeven point.

Table: Break-even Analysis

8.3 Projected Profit and Loss

The following table and charts will indicate Projected Profit and Loss.

Table: Profit and Loss

Pro Forma Profit and Loss

Year 1   Year 2   Year 3

Sales

Direct Cost of

Other

Costs of Sales

Total Cost of Sales

Gross Margin

Gross Margin

Expenses Payroll

Sales and Marketing and Other Expenses

Depreciation

Rent

Utilities

Insurance

Payroll Taxes

Other

Total Operating Expenses

Profit before Interest and

Interest Expense

Taxes Incurred

Net Profit

Net Profit/Sales

8.4 Projected Cash Flow

The following table and chart will indicate Projected Cash Flow.

8.6 Business Ratios

The following table provides information regarding business ratios specific to ABC Data Entry Service as well as ratios specific to the data entry industry. Please note that making a comparison of a data entry specialist and an administrative service consultant is a difficult comparison. It is expected that the ratios will be quite different between the two as a DEA is a home based, in this case single individual business.

SUMMARY

We hope the information provided in this guide has inspired you to get on the path to entrepreneurship. While working as your own boss can be challenging at times, it is also extremely rewarding. Your success and good business decisions benefit you, and not someone else. You will gain experience and confidence that you may never have known that you even had. Developing your own business from scratch and watching it grow and succeed is very rewarding. Once your data entry business is well-established, you may even want to expand beyond churches into other types of businesses. You can also offer additional services on top of your data entry work. Just remember to start small and always be professional.

Your skills, and of course your determination, may dictate what other services you want to offer however there is always room for growth and improvement. You don't need to offer ALL of these services to have a successful business and many operators only handle data entries but the potential exists. Here is a list of others services you might consider offering. If you do not have the skills there's no reason you cannot learn them and add them to your business in the future:

Word processing
Tape transcription
Phone-in dictation
Desktop publishing
Spreadsheet design
College papers and reports
Telephone answering
Mail receiving and forwarding
Packing and shipping
Database/mailing list management
Bookkeeping, check preparation and billing
Resume preparation
Proofreading
Print brokering
Fax sending and receiving

Photocopying
Notary
Internet research
Web page design and maintenance
Event planning
Consulting
Training

Whatever you do, have fun and be creative! You can start part-time and easily make a healthy second income. Good luck and enjoy your new career.

Visit www.crutcherproducts.com for more career and skills information

ABOUT THE AUTHOR

G. Crutcher Dutch is an author, entrepreneur and an infopreneur. She resides in Texas with her two dogs, laptop and tons of reference books. Her many years of working in the Government, private industry and running her own businesses has given her the knowledge that she puts in informational books.

Made in the USA
Las Vegas, NV
14 April 2024

88671918R00059